Personal Data Protection

The 1984 Act and its Implications

J M Court

PUBLISHED BY NCC PUBLICATIONS

British Library Cataloguing in Publication Data

Court, J. M.
    Personal data protection.
    1. Data protection
    I. Title   II. National Computing Centre
    001.64'42   K3264.C65

    ISBN 0-85012-424-7

First published in 1984 by:

NCC Publications, The National Computing Centre Ltd, Oxford Road, Manchester M1 7ED, England.

Typeset in 11pt Times Roman by UPS Blackburn Ltd, 76-80 Northgate, Blackburn, Lancashire; and printed by Hobbs the Printers of Southampton.

ISBN 0-85012-424-7

Contents

1 Introduction

This book describes the factors which contribute to the protection of financial data on computer files, and explores the extent to which these factors also contribute to the protection of personal data in computing, word processing and other information technology systems. Other aspects of personal data protection are also examined in detail, in relation to legal and other requirements.

The scope and impact of data protection law are examined, but the book is not confined to a discussion of legislation. It also considers what is important in general in data protection and what is important in particular in relation to all categories of sensitive data (including personal data, financial data, etc).

The book also shows how data protection can assist and improve, rather than inhibit, the use of computer systems. It examines how requirements for data protection may be built into all stages of system development or acquisition, and into the operational use of computers. The need to integrate manual procedures with the use of computer systems is not overlooked.

The following chapters are written largely from the point of view of commercial organisations, but this is only for convenience. The matters considered are applicable, mutatis mutandis, to *all* users of computer systems holding personal or other sensitive or valuable data.

Section numbers quoted in the text and in the footnotes are references to the Data Protection Act 1984.

7

2 The Legal Framework

INTRODUCTION – THE DATA PROTECTION ACT 1984

The Data Protection Act, finally enacted in 1984, is directed towards the protection of personal data (which it defines as "data consisting of information which relates to a living individual who can be identified from the information, or from that and other information in the possession of the data user"). This definition allows little scope for compromise.

The Data Protection law applies *only* to computer-based records. If records are maintained clerically they are completely outside the scope of this law.

The purpose of this legislation is stated as being:

(i) to implement the proposals set out in the White Paper on Data Protection published in April 1982 (Cmnd. 8539);

(ii) to enable the United Kingdom to ratify the European Convention (which the UK has signed) for the Protection of Individuals with regard to Automatic Processing of Personal Data.

Of these purposes (which in practical terms are more or less identical, since the White Paper incorporates the main features of the European Convention), the second is apparently regarded by the government as the more urgent.

The law establishes a Data Protection Registrar, who will maintain a register of personal data users and computer bureaux and have powers to ensure that personal data is used in accordance with stated data protection principles. It sets up an Appeal Tribunal for data users; and gives data subjects certain legal rights, including a (sometimes qualified) right of access to their personal data, and in certain circumstances a right to compensation if such data is misused. We will return in due course to a detailed consideration of a number of these matters.

This legislation was first published as a Bill in December 1982. The publication of the Bill was something of an anti-climax, after two Committees of Enquiry and at least ten years of discussion about the need for, and the possible contents of, such legislation. This discussion involved such bodies as the National Computing Centre, the British Computer Society and the Institute of Data Processing Managers, as well as the legal profession, the medical profession, the police and civil liberties groups. Only after the Bill had been published did many people begin to realise that such legislation was actually possible – and reactions were mixed.

Many decision-makers and opinion-framers did not see the need for such legislation and resented the implication that they and their organisations were not responsible users of data. Also, many small business people found the prospect of such legislation (like that dealing with PAYE, VAT and statutory sick pay) irksome, and considered that they would almost certainly find it oppressive and time-consuming.

Both categories of people expressed opposition, forcing the government to change the scope of the legislation. The loss of the 1982 Bill because of the General Election of June 1983 did not really affect this process, but did make it possible for the Home Office to incorporate changes into a new version of the Bill which could then be introduced, with minimum embarrassment, into a new Parliament.

One of the changes made at this stage was that people keeping computerised records for accounting purposes were (generally speaking) exempted from any requirement to register as data users, or to allow the subjects of those records to have access to their contents. People using computers to calculate staff pay and pensions were similarly (generally speaking) exempted.

However, this issue is by no means as clear-cut as would have been desirable. The use of personal data held for the purpose of calculating amounts payable by way of remuneration or pensions in respect of service in any employment or office is exempt from registration under the Act, and the subject of that data has no right of access to it. But this does not apply to personnel records – so if you use the same files both in your payroll calculations and in the maintenance of your personnel records this exemption, strictly speaking, *does not apply*.

This is almost bound to be the case if you use an integrated database – so the use of an integrated database for personnel records is almost bound to remove the exemption. Yet the use of such databases is growing more widely – so what price the exemption?

The same exemption is also available when data is used for the purpose of keeping accounts relating to any business or other activity conducted by the data user, or of keeping records of purchases, sales or other transactions. Again, if you use the same database of stock records for both accounting and other purposes (eg production control, stock control), or the same customers' database for both accounting and credit rating purposes, the exemption for accounting purposes is likely to be removed by the non-applicability of its exemption to the other purposes.

Further comments will be made on these matters in later chapters.

LEGAL REQUIREMENTS FOR GENERAL DATA PROTECTION

Many people resisted the whole idea of data protection, and exerted particular pressure to secure the exemption of accounting and payroll records. It was felt that there is already a framework of laws which protects business data in general and accounting records in particular. Such laws do not ensure the integrity of personal data specifically, or any element of data completely, but do together help to ensure that all data (including, therefore, personal data) is reasonably accurate and reasonably well-controlled. It is important not to underestimate the scope or importance of these general legal requirements (the most significant are considered below).

The Law of Libel

It is libellous to cause personal damage by publishing inaccurate information (for example, if you tell a debt collector that Mr. A has owed you £1,000 for the past six months, when in fact he paid you in advance, and Mr. A is financially or socially embarrassed as a result, Mr. A can sue you). Publication of inaccurate personal information as the output of a computer system is certainly within the scope of this law.

Forgeries, Theft or Unauthorised Release of Customers' Funds

If a bank pays over your money on the basis of a forged instrument, it must give you a refund. The same applies to the use of your cheque card, or credit card, if you have reported it missing as soon as you discover its loss. If the use of these facilities is connected with the operation of the bank's computer systems (as it normally is), the bank is under an obligation to its customers and share-holders. A sound system of internal controls over its customers' computer records (which in this case are both important personal data and significant accounting information) is required in order to minimise the chance of successful forgeries, thefts or unauthor-ised release of funds. Similar considerations apply to incorrect or unauthorised standing-order payments or direct debits.

Need for Audit of Limited Liability Company

All limited companies have to be audited by specifically qualified professional auditors. The auditors have to report on the truth and fairness of all sets of accounts showing the state of affairs of a company (its assets and liabilities), and its profit or loss for the period covered by the accounts. In coming to their conclusions on these matters, the auditors normally have to evaluate the com-pany's systems of internal controls, including those which seek to maximise the security, confidentiality, accuracy and completeness of the company's computer records, in so far as these incorporate accounting records or records of assets or liabilities.

3 Legal Obligations

Apart from any of the matters to be discussed in later chapters, there are specific obligations under the Data Protection legislation to which you must pay attention if you hold any personal data for non-exempt purposes[1]:

— apply for registration as a data user within 6 months of the date fixed[2] by the Secretary of State for the law to come into force. You are not prohibited from processing any data until six months after this date, although from the outset you must observe the data protection principles set out in the Data Protection law (see Chapter 5). You are obliged to register:

— your name and address;

— a description of the personal data to be held by you and of the purpose or purposes for which the data is to be held or used;

— a description of the source or sources from which you intend or may wish to obtain the data or the information to be contained in the data;

— a description of any person or persons to whom you intend or may wish to disclose the data;

— the names or a description of any countries or territories outside the United Kingdom to which you

[1] Exemptions are discussed in Chapter 7.
[2] Still to be fixed, following the enactment of the legislation. (Unfortunately, you will have to pay a fee.)

intend or may wish directly or indirectly to transfer the data;

— one or more addresses for the receipt of requests from data subjects for access to the data.

If you are *only* a computer bureau, you need *only* register your name and address, but you must *also* make sure that those who use your services are themselves properly registered as users.

You are deemed to run a "computer bureau" if you provide others with services in respect of data, either

— as agent for other persons[1] (ie you run computer systems on their behalf), or

— you allow other persons the use of your equipment to run their own computer systems.

If you *use* a computer bureau, you are still a data user and must register accordingly – ie you must register *all* of the above-mentioned details.

— do not process data, after registration (or after six months from the date to be fixed), except in accordance with the terms of your application to be registered. The Registrar cannot strike you off the register (by means of a "de-registration notice"), for any reason whatsoever, until 2 years have elapsed since the date fixed by the relevant Secretary of State (in this instance the Home Secretary); but

[1] In the opinion of the author, statutory auditors, performing computer audit techniques by processing their clients' files on their own (the auditors') computer, are operating as a computer bureau and should register accordingly. Correspondingly, clients may wish to register "audit" as one of the purposes for which personal data may be used (for example in payroll systems) – though for other reasons, to be mentioned later, this is not strictly necessary. After all, if the *client* is registered as the "user" of the data – in the sense of controlling it – then the *auditor* must be something different. In fact, the auditor *must not be* the user of the data in the sense of controlling it: an audit is conducted to discover whether or not the data is correct – not to control it.

— he may seek to take action against you, subsequently, in the light of adverse information obtained about you during those 2 years;

— even during these 2 years, he may impose specific requirements on you, or indicate an intention to strike you off the register, by means of an order taking effect at the conclusion of that period.

— do not transfer information, after registration, to another data user outside the UK except in accordance with the terms of your registration, and do not contravene the terms of any notice from the Registrar (a "transfer prohibition notice") which places restrictions on your right to do so. Again, the Registrar cannot make such a notice stick for 2 years from the date fixed by the Secretary of State, but it would be more prudent to observe the spirit rather than the letter if the Registrar serves such a notice, pending expiry of that period, at any earlier data.

— allow any applicant, on payment of the specified fee, to have full details of the data which you are holding about him/her[1]. Do not allow him/her to have access to any other data. You have 40 days in which to comply with a request for data access.

— do not allow anyone to have access to data about anyone else who has not consented to this[2]. This is an overriding principle: you can even refuse to allow an applicant to have access to his or her own personal data if this is impossible without inadvertently revealing someone else's. (But make sure it is actually impossible, not just inconvenient.) You must yourself be satisfied of the identity of a person who applies for access to personal data.

If you break any of these rules, the Registrar can issue an "enforcement notice", requiring you to comply with them.

---

[1] Again, provided you are not exempt from this requirement – see Chapter 7.

[2] Yet again, there are exemptions – see Chapter 7.

Renewal of registration will be required from time to time, probably every three years from the date of first registration. *Note particularly that* if the Registrar issues a de-registration notice and thus strikes you off the register, you commit a criminal offence if you continue to process any data by means of a computer system. This also applies if the Registrar refuses to register you in the first place (and still refuses to do so after the initial 2 years have elapsed since the date fixed by the Secretary of State), or if the Registrar refuses to re-register you.

You can appeal against any of these notices from the Registrar (ie de-registration notices, transfer prohibition notices and enforcement notices). Appeals must be made to the Data Protection Tribunal against any of these notices, or against a refusal by the Registrar to register you in the first place. The notices will all contain details of appeal rights.

The Data Protection Tribunal is a panel consisting of lawyers, computing specialists, computer users and laymen appointed by the Lord Chancellor and the Secretary of State. There is still a right of appeal from this Tribunal to the High Court (Court of Session in Scotland).

The Registrar's office, like all bureaucracies, will have a tendency to try to maximise its influence, and is therefore likely to put a strict construction on the meaning of "personal" and the scope of "personal data", and on the other requirements of the data protection law. In other words, you will not get away with non-compliance because your use of personal data is trivial or incidental, or because it is tedious to monitor your various uses of it. On the other hand, the Registrar will be responsible and reasonable in his enforcement of the provisions of the law, and will act with strict impartiality. For example, the Registrar will not take any action against you if you refuse to give someone (perhaps a disgruntled employee) access to some trivial item of personal data if it is quite clear that this person is not really interested in the data but just wants to cause you inconvenience.

The Registrar is the enforcement officer for the personal data protection law. Private individuals cannot seek to enforce the law. They can only seek damages against you in the civil courts. If you have caused them no damage then your non-compliance with the data protection law, or the data protection principles, is not going to help them. The Registrar, conversely, cannot sue you in the civil courts but can either prosecute you in the criminal courts or seek evidence against you. If the Registrar seeks evidence against you, you may (provided a circuit judge approves – in Scotland a sheriff and in Northern Ireland a county court judge) get raided by the Registrar's staff[1]. You *do* – normally, at least – get at least seven days' notice in writing of the Registrar's intention to apply to the court for permission to raid you, and you *do* have a right to be heard in court yourself. You *do* have a right to a receipt for anything seized (eg your computer files) and you *do* have a right to a copy of anything seized (eg your computer files) provided that this does not cause undue delay.

On the other hand, the Registrar's men *do* have the right to use "such reasonable force as may be necessary". You can of course always let them in voluntarily, when they first approach you, and avoid the need for applications to courts. If you have nothing to hide, this is the best thing to do.

Indeed, if you find that some aspect of the information on your computer files is wrong, then correct it at once. Do not wait for any request, or statutory requirement, to do so. Incorrect data can only prejudice the proper management of your business or other activities – *it is in your own interests* to see that your data is as accurate and up-to-date as possible. If information is an *asset*, and has a *value*, you are that much the poorer if the information you are using is wrong.

[1] Schedule 4.

4 Who Uses Data and Why

RESPONSIBILITY FOR DATA

The Data Protection legislation (section 1(5)) defines a data user as a person who "holds" data, and states that a person holds data if that person (either alone or jointly or in common with other persons) *controls* the contents and use of the data (my *italics*).

Presumably, you control data if:

— you decide if, when and how it should be processed;

— it is freely available to you for your use;

— access to the data by you is unrestricted, either by the system itself, or by the processing methods adopted in relation to that data.

This is why data which existed only on files maintained in a computer system as strictly temporary working storage files (scratch pad, update or pipeline files) would surely not be subject to the provisions of the Data Protection legislation (though no doubt this would require both legal argument and a close examination of the details of the case). However, in a very real sense you would not "control" this data. This would particularly be the case if you were using a turnkey system which you did not possess the skill to modify. It would also be the case if your operating procedures and disciplinary rules prohibited the modification of a system, except under controlled conditions, even if some members of your staff possessed the necessary skills.

This raises the important question of who the "person" is who "holds" data. If you are a sole trader, or a private individual, then obviously it is you. If you are the UK Administration Director of a large multinational conglomerate, with numerous data processing personnel, some reporting to you and some to other directors, and with large numbers of other people using computers which you do not even know about, then the question is more vexed.

The Data Protection law makes it clear (section 20(1)) that a body corporate (a legal "person") is liable for its offences under the legislation. However, the same sub-section also states that any director, manager, company secretary or any similar officer (or anyone purporting to be such an officer) is equally liable if he or she consented to or connived at the offence. Such a person will be "punished accordingly".

So if you are in a position within the management of a body corporate to consent to, or connive at, an offence under the Data Protection law, you are effectively in the same position as a person who controls data – whether you actually *do* control it or not. This principle presumably falls over into other circumstances, so that there is a fourth formulation of the essential criteria for "controlling" data – ie that you control data:

— if you are in a position to consent to, or connive at, its misuse.

Although the concept of "controlling" data is included within the Data Protection law and is therefore specifically intended to apply to *personal* data on computer files, there seems no reason why it should not also be regarded as applicable, more generally, to the maintenance of all types of such data.

You may feel that in most cases it would be difficult to identify a single individual who "controlled" a particular piece of data. If so, it is worth asking why. Any particular material piece of data should have an owner, responsible for its initial and continuing accuracy, and for the way in which it is used. This was recognised as a principle of sound database processing long before the Data Protection law was introduced. If this principle is not implemented, it means that the management of data processing is, to some extent at least, sloppy. In turn this means that the results of data processing are open to avoidable error. Apart from the fact that avoidable error can, in certain conditions, include fraud, it can also (without any fraudulent intent or activity) cause both perpetrator and victim inconvenience, frustration, waste of time, and in certain circumstances direct monetary loss.

DATA DICTIONARY

It is therefore good for your business, quite apart from being your legal responsibility (in respect of personal data) under the Data Protection law, to identify an owner of each material piece of data, and to make him or her specifically responsible for its accuracy. This person will then be in a position to specify who else should use that data, and why.

These characteristics can often be incorporated in a "data dictionary", maintained by software (or occasionally otherwise). The contents of a data dictionary should include, at least, details of:

— the identity of each type of data recorded on the relevant computer file;

— the characteristics of that type of data (eg numeric or non-numeric, length, format, access keys);

— the owner of data elements of that type (ie who is entitled to enter, update and delete such data elements – this will be the person recognised by the Data Protection law as the one who primarily "controls" the data). This will also prevent conflicts of understanding on this point which are almost certain to arise (for example between the payroll and personnel supervisors over employees' records or between the sales manager and the accountant over customers' records) if specific decisions are not made about primary responsibility for particular types of data;

— restrictions on right of access to that type of data;

— restrictions on right of amendment to that type of data.

DATA ADMINISTRATION

One of the problems associated with data dictionaries, and other aspects of database systems and technology, is an unfortunate confusion of terminologies, which involves different concepts of the scope of database administration, and the multiplication of associated definitions.

The exact division of responsibilities to be carried out by various officials in the normal course of events depends to a considerable extent on, firstly, the exact nature of the data to be processed and, secondly, the methods of data control already in operation. However, administration of data in the context of a database system is probably best considered as two distinct activities:

— database administration, having responsibility for database design and the integration of users' requirements;

— data administration, having responsibility for data maintenance, analysis and accuracy.

A database administrator maintains a database in such a way that it can be accessed without difficulty by any user program, regardless of what changes are made to the physical attributes of the database.

Certain activities of a database administrator may be regarded as simply data control and file maintenance. Such activities will involve the planning of database file structures, together with other activities, in relation to the planning of database systems, undertaken in conjunction with the systems analysts concerned. Particularly, it must be determined at the outset of database implementation which of the rules of the real world are relevant to the subjects about which data is held on the database. These rules must be converted into statements of logical relationships in accordance with which all combinations of data on the database, as far as it is possible to determine, must be initially consistent, and must remain consistent after any number of authorised updates. The database administrator should not normally define or prepare the programs which impose these constraints on the database, but it ought also to be part of the administration function to ensure that, as far as possible, there is always a detailed correspondence between the real world, as represented by the relevant logical relationships, and the contents of the database. In any event, it is clear that the maintenance of file consistency is one of the most significant aspects of overall data protection.

Certain other activities of the database administrator may be seen as simply what used to be called maintenance programming. For example, the database administrator will necessarily have responsibility for maintaining the continuing accuracy of the database documentation, and of consistency between the physical characteristics of each database and the data definitions within the various application programs; and for the amendment of programs, if necessary, to take account of any alteration to such physical characteristics.

All other data administration functions should normally be the responsibility of users of computer systems: for example, the daily, weekly or monthly control over the completeness and accuracy of, say, processed sales transactions, and the corresponding accuracy of the balances on the sales ledger account.

It is also important, however, that the responsibilities of the users should be co-ordinated in relation to the maintenance of information on any file which is common to a number of applications (for example, the address, credit limit, statistical information and sales reference information which may be used not only in the sales accounting system, but also in the order recording, sales commission, regional management information and credit control applications). This could be the responsibility of a data administrator independent of the users of any of those systems.

5 Data-Protection Principles

INTRODUCTION

There are various types of data that need to be protected – for legal, practical or commercial reasons – and identical mechanisms for protection can be used in all cases.

PERSONAL DATA (required to be protected by law)

Protection is required for any item which relates to the life or activities of an identifiable individual, except in connection with the calculation of pay or pension, or the maintenance of accounting information on a personal business basis; ie any record on a file, including:

— a person's name;

— a person's current address, or

— a person's public identity number (eg National Insurance number, Medical Card number, passport number);

— a person's unique status or position.

OTHER PRIVATE DATA

Other types of private data requiring protection include:

— scientific formulae or data constituting a trade or business secret;

— indexes, on computer files, containing references to other data files containing personal, private or commercially valuable data;

— computer programs of commercial value.

OTHER COMMERCIAL DATA

This may also sometimes fall within the scope of the Data Protection law – or at least it would be unwise to suppose that it did not (see Chapter 2). Here the primary motive for protection is commercial prudence. Commercial data requiring protection includes:

— payroll and pension records;

— accounting and management records, including records of:

    — amounts payable and receivable (purchases and sales ledgers);

    — cash transactions;

    — purchases and sales (including records of VAT inputs and outputs);

    — stock (inventory) and warehouse location records;

    — production control;

    — budgetary control.

PROTECTION PRINCIPLES

As has been codified elsewhere[1], there are thirteen intrinsic principles contained in the Younger (1972) and Lindop (1978) Reports on personal data privacy, and in the European Convention and OECD Guidelines on data protection.

System Design Principles

Most (though not all) of these principles have been directly incorporated into the UK legislation on personal data privacy. Some, however, apply to the *design* of all computer systems: they represent sound concepts of system design and implementation, *quite*

[1] NCC Computer Security Series, *The External Auditor as Privacy Inspector* (see bibliography).

apart from the matter of security. Five of these wider principles (which thus apply to systems dealing with *both* personal data *and* other forms of sensitive data) may be identified:

— data should only be held for a clearly specified purpose; it should not be used for any other purpose without appropriate authorisation. (N.B. This implies the adequate documentation of the purposes of the system, the form of the data being used by it, and the way in which this data is processed);

— data collected and held on the files of a system should be the minimum necessary to achieve a specified purpose. (N.B. This may be achieved by technical manipulations of data such as normalisation (whereby, in a database context, the duplication of occurrences of all data elements – including personal and other sensitive data – is minimised). It may also be achieved by more general methods, such as close attention, at the outset, to how the needs of different potential users of a proposed system are related);

— all data retained on the files of a system should be as accurate as reasonably practicable. (N.B. This may often be achieved by file monitoring procedures to validate the format and content of data being used to update the files, and its consistency with data already present on those files);

— data should only be maintained within the files of a system for as long as necessary. (N.B. Procedures for purging files, as well as maintaining back-up, are important in this connection);

— access to data should be confined to those who have been authorised to access it. (N.B. This principle may often, but not necessarily, be achieved by password-controlled access to files and programmed functions).

All these matters are considered in greater detail in the next chapter.

Personal Data Protection Principles

The eight principles laid down in the Data Protection legislation

(Schedule 1) are specific to the protection of personal data. Again, however, they also have a more general relevance: some of them are either explicit or implicit in the general principles just considered.

The first seven of these principles are as follows (they apply to data *users* only – not to people running computer bureaux and processing other people's data):

— the information to be contained in personal data shall be obtained fairly and lawfully, and personal data shall also be processed fairly and lawfully. (N.B. Readers may safely ignore the distinction between "data" and the "information" which such data "contains").

   The legislation declares that, in determining whether information was obtained fairly, regard shall be had to the method by which it was obtained, including in particular whether any person from whom it was obtained was deceived or misled as to the purpose or purposes for which it is to be held.

   It notes that information shall in any event be treated as obtained fairly if it is obtained from a person who is authorised or required by or under any enactment (or international treaty) to supply it.

   This is a relief, for example, to statutory auditors, acting under the Companies Acts and similar legislation: it means that they can still perform audit interrogations of personal data on their clients' files, even though their clients may not have registered the auditors as people to whom such personal data was to be transferred.

— personal data shall be held only for one or more specified and lawful purposes (the specified purposes will be the ones specified to the Registrar).

— personal data held for any purpose or purposes shall not be used or disclosed in any manner incompatible with that purpose or those purposes.

— personal data held for any purpose or purposes shall be adequate, relevant and not excessive in relation to that purpose or those purposes.

— personal data shall be accurate and, where necessary, kept up-to-date. The legislation does include a section (Section 22) which modifies this statement, to ensure that data users who do all that is reasonable to maintain the accuracy and immediacy of data will not be penalised if, even so, it is found to be inaccurate.

— personal data held for any purpose or purposes shall not be kept for longer than is necessary for that purpose or those purposes.

— an individual shall be entitled:

(a) at reasonable intervals and without undue delay or expense:

— to be informed by any data user whether he holds personal data of which that individual is the subject; and

— to have access to any such data held by a user;

(b) where appropriate to have such data corrected or erased. It is not entirely clear what constitutes a "reasonable interval" – the legislation says that it depends on circumstances, including the nature of the data and how often it is changed.

The eighth principle applies to both data users and operators of computer bureaux, and in some respects it is the most far-reaching. It requires *all* those who run computer systems dealing with personal data to adopt appropriate security measures against:

— *unauthorised access* to data;

— *unauthorised alteration or destruction* of data;

— *unauthorised disclosure* of data;

— *accidental loss or destruction* of data.

This principle does not mention unauthorised insertion of data in the first place. Otherwise, it incorporates into law a requirement for the imposition of most if not all of the sorts of internal controls

which auditors, security consultants and the professional computing bodies have for a long time advocated as unavoidably necessary
in the context of:

— all accounting systems;

— all other systems using data which has a crucial or commercial value,

whatever the size of those systems.

These controls must be essentially similar to the controls described by the accountancy profession, in connection with financial
and accounting systems, as "application controls" and "general
controls" (the latter often also described as "installation controls"
or "organisational controls").

The accountancy profession defines:

— *application controls* as covering the transactions and stand-
ing data used by each application. They are, therefore,
specific to each application. The objectives of application
controls are to ensure the completeness and accuracy of the
accounting records and the validity of the entries therein
resulting from both computer and manual processing. Some
application controls (such as the checking of batch total
reconciliations) may be performed manually; others (such
as input edit checks included in computer programs) may be
performed by computer;

— *general controls* as covering the environment within which
applications are developed, maintained and operated, and
within which application controls operate. The objectives
of general controls are to ensure the integrity of application
development and implementation, program and data files,
and computer operations. Some general controls (such as
restricting physical access to data files) may be performed
manually; others (such as providing password protection
for program files) may be performed by computer.

Such controls, and the procedures by which they may be implemented, have to be related to the principles incorporated in the
data protection legislation (see Chapter 6). A few crucial points,
however, are worth noting at the outset:

— application controls and general/installation controls relate to both:

    — transactions data (data regularly input);

    — master file data (permanent or semi-permanent data such as customers' names and addresses; details of fulfilment of long-term building contracts to date; bills of materials for standard products; VAT or personal tax records).

— such controls relate to both programs and data files – simply because both are maintained on magnetic file media. A computer makes no distinction, at its architectural level, between programs and files. This distinction is made by the programs themselves.

— such controls may be exercised both:

    — physically (eg at night you can lock away your terminals, data files and programs, and keep your printer in a special place);

    — logically (eg you can preclude access to programs and data files by means of programs – often called access control software[1]).

---

[1] Clearly, this involves an infinite regress problem: there must be at least one program to which no other program can preclude access, and this program must permit access to all other programs – otherwise you could be put in a position where you would not be able to access any program at all. This means that at least one person within a computer installation must have access, via this master program, to all other programs, and therefore to all other data files, This fact is well known, but its *logical* character is often overlooked – in other words, that there is no means by which you can avoid it.

6 Data-Protection Procedures

GENERAL

Because the principles which apply to the protection of personal data also apply to other forms of data which need protecting – apart from any legal obligation to do so – it is appropriate to consider protection procedures and their implications in the light of these principles. This consideration now follows. Each of the principles is analysed and discussed with reference to the factors to which users should have regard in seeking to comply with it.

Principle 1 – Information shall be obtained and processed fairly and lawfully:

— *Information shall be obtained fairly*

Do not mislead anyone, either within or outside your organisation, about why you need or are intending to process data.

Make sure you only obtain the information you actually need for the operation of your system. This involves a *good initial feasibility study* and *good system design*. Note that, *quite apart from questions of data protection*, this is in the interests of efficient and cost-effective processing.

— *Information shall be processed fairly*

You should only process information, obtained for a particular purpose, for that purpose. Frame your objectives for the use of information *sufficiently widely before you obtain it*.

Implement procedures to minimise the risk that data can be processed in unauthorised ways: for example, keep file media secure and limit on-line access to sensitive programmed procedures (if any, eg updating reference data such as addresses, credit limits, loan facilities and stock prices).

— *Information shall be obtained lawfully*

Do not process any data which has been obtained directly from any individual, or from any other organisation, unless you are satisfied that you have explicit authority to do so. If another organisation or any other third party supplies you with personal information, make sure that they have recorded, on the public data register, their intention to do so. (N.B. This requirement is waived if you are entitled to obtain the information under the terms of any statute, such as the Companies Acts).

— *Information shall be processed lawfully*

Implement procedures to minimise the risks of:

— theft of computer time;

— theft of other computer facilities, including file media;

— theft of programs or data files;

— breaches of software licences and agreements;

— breaches of software copyright and intellectual property rights.

Thus, for example, ensure that:

— use of computer time is logged (by program or clerically, or by some appropriate combination);

— use of file media (disks, diskettes, cassettes, tapes) is similarly logged;

— terminals cannot be used indiscriminately to gain access to the contents of files or programs in order to copy them. Make sure that access to relevant utility programs is suitably restricted (for example, by removing them from your system altogether and loading them under controlled circumstances only when required);

— software packages (both system software and application software) are not used on machines for which they are not licensed. Observe the requirements of software licence agreements, while making sure that you do not enter into onerous contracts (eg ensure that you do not lose the right to use software if there is a dispute with its licensor, or in the event of the licensor going into liquidation or receivership: these possibilities may be somewhat remote, but can be very inconvenient if they eventuate);

— no use is made of any program which you may have good reason to believe has been copied, from the source of its ownership (either directly or with only minor modifications), and marketed, without permission. There are three common indicators that this may be the case:

  — the software supplier will appear in no reputable list of suppliers, and probably not even in the telephone directory;

  — the software will generate output or displays which show indications of the removal of some third party's name (sometimes it is even still there);

  — no support whatsoever will be offered, or be forthcoming, from the supplier.

Principle 2 – Data shall be held for specified and lawful purposes:

— *Data shall be held for specified purposes*

The significance of documentation in this context has already been mentioned. This principle will not be realised unless you document your system so that you actually know the characteristics of the data you are using. Use a data dictionary if this is appropriate.

Despite a reluctance among many software designers and suppliers (of both large-scale and micro-based software) to provide adequate documentation of the systems which they develop, documentation is still essential to a full understanding of what a system does. This may be done by means of such aids to users as screen prompts and "help" facilities, as well as full explanations presented on a screen instead of on paper – just as long as they *are* full explanations and not just sops to the supplier's conscience.

In the absence of any reason to the contrary, "documentation" (in the wide sense mentioned above) should include (as a minimum) information about the following functions of a piece of software – whether it is tailored or packaged, for use with a large or small-scale computer, and whether produced in-house or purchased:

—   a general statement of its objectives and functions;

—   descriptions of its inputs and files, and descriptions or statements of the key calculations and logical functions performed by it;

—   operating instructions for its use;

—   a statement of any regular routine procedures which ought to be associated with its use (eg file re-organisation when full);

—   a statement of the recovery procedures which ought to be implemented in connection with its use;

—   a statement of the control procedures which ought to be implemented in connection with its use. Matters relating to such control procedures will be discussed in more detail below – this is the aspect of system documentation which is frequently the most deficient. The NCC publication *Accounting Software Controls* (1983) notes (p 15) (in connection with packaged accounting software, but the same is true generally) that such controls may be exercised by means of:

    —   clerical or independent mechanised control procedures, required to enable proper accounting control to be exercised by reference to output reports or visual displays;

— programmed controls designed to impose direct control over aspects of the operation of programmed procedures or the continuing integrity of data.

The same publication recommends (p 13) that evidence of the operation of such controls should be reported as regular printed or displayed output, and the documentation and/or training in the use of significant computer systems should advise users and potential users that the examination of output should always form an element in the clerical accounting control procedures.

Documentation is the Cinderella of software implementation procedures: it deserves more frequent visits to the ball. Maybe the data protection law will help in this.

— *Data shall be held for lawful purposes*

Over and above the procedures carried out by data administrators (see previous chapters), it is almost certainly a good idea for the chief executive of any organisation (or someone specifically nominated by the chief executive) to consider the documentation of every computer application, and every computer file and record, and to assent to the legitimacy of the purposes for which the data is held, and the need for the maintenance of the data in order to fulfil those purposes.

In so far as "lawful" embraces "fairness" and "legitimacy", as well as authorisation, the procedures suggested under Principle 1, above, are also relevant.

Principle 3 – Data shall not be used in any manner incompatible with the purposes for which it is held.

Apart from the procedures suggested in connection with Principle 2, which are also relevant to Principle 3, the following procedures are also relevant:

— initial testing of the facilities of all newly-installed systems –

whether packaged or otherwise – by the *users* of those systems. This should be done to ensure that the programs which are to process the users' data do so in accordance with the users' pre-specified requirements.

— periodical retesting, by users, of these facilities. This procedure is recommended in order to ensure that the original functions of a program are not subsequently modified in an unapproved way (whether unintentionally or maliciously) by:

   — the direct effect of single large-scale program amendments;

   — the indirect cumulative effect of a large number of small-scale program amendments;

   — the introduction or re-introduction of erroneous or superseded versions of a program package or set of programs.

Principles 4 and 6 – Data shall be, in relation to the purposes for which it is held, adequate, relevant, not excessive and held for no longer than necessary (the sixth principle).

These principles are rather more pious than helpful. It is significant that the data protection legislation (despite representations from a number of sources during its passage through Parliament) does not give any additional guidance on how they should be interpreted.

A few points in connection with these principles, however, are important:

— *Data shall be adequate to its purposes*. In order to achieve this, make sure that you maintain organised records of the contents of files – a file library. (Do this, however small-scale your files may be – floppy disks can get confused, if anything, even more easily than more imposing file media.) If you use a fixed disk, you still need to be sure you know what it contains. Important files should be copied for back-up purposes at sufficiently frequent intervals.

— *Data shall be relevant to its purposes, and not excessive*.

Achievement of this principle involves:

— regular purging of files;

— regular review, by the chief executive or a specified nominee, of master file data containing permanent and semi-permanent reference information. This review should incorporate the identification of possibly redundant or avoidably duplicated data (N.B. If such a review can be assisted by software, so much the better);

— adherence to, and similar review of, procedures for copying and backing up files and programs, and recording the whereabouts of file media.

— *Data shall be held on computer files for no longer than necessary*. In many instances, no clear policies are ever formulated about how long information, in whatever form, should be retained within a commercial organisation or privately. Legal requirements about minimum periods for the retention of different categories of information are often obscure, and in any case are not the subject of this book.

Apart from legal requirements, however, this principle involves value judgements as to the nature of "necessity" in individual circumstances of data usage. Such value judgements could never be generalised.

So be pragmatic. Ask "why" you need to retain any particular piece of information. If the answer is "there might still be a query about it", then keep it, however old it is.

Incidentally, a Home Office minister has made it clear that information can be retained for historical purposes, even if it was not originally collected with this in mind. This is entirely in accordance with the Data Protection Act which states (Schedule I, Part II, 7) that:

"Where personal data are (sic) held for historical, statistical or research purposes and not used in such a way that damage or distress is, or is likely to be, caused to any data subject –

(a) the information contained in the data shall not be regarded
for the purposes of the first principle as obtained unfairly by
reason only that its use for any such purpose was not disclosed when it was obtained; and

(b) the data may, notwithstanding the sixth principle, be kept
indefinitely."

The precise point of the sixth principle thus remains elusive.

Principle 5 – Data shall be accurate and up-to-date.

— a great many considerations relevant to this principle are
dealt with under the heading of Principle 8 (below);

— one procedure which is particularly relevant to this principle, however, is the periodical examination, by users, of the
contents of computer files containing sensitive information,
to confirm the continuing integrity of this information. If
the volume of such information is high (as is frequently the
case), examination of an unbiased and sufficient sample of
it will normally reveal at least one example of any generic
errors which it may contain. (N.B. The number of items to
be examined in order to achieve a sufficient sample is open
to a lot of highly detailed and academic discussion and
argument. However, 50 items each containing an occurr-
ence of the attribute which is being examined for correctness – eg wage rates included in employees' personnel and
payroll records – should normally be sufficient).

This procedure is recommended, although it is undoub-
tedly tedious and time-consuming, because the quality and
accuracy of data on computer files may well degenerate
over a period of time, for a number of reasons, including:

— the direct effect of single large-scale program amendments;

— the indirect cumulative effect of a large number of
small-scale program amendments;

— operational errors;

— errors caused by the side-effects of features of the
operating system, database management software or

network control software.

— the data protection legislation makes it clear that if you do all that is *reasonable* to ensure that data is accurate and up-to-date you will not be faulted for the application of this principle. You will surely have done all that is reasonable if you do all that is suggested in this monograph.

Principle 7 – An individual shall be entitled:

— to be informed whether personal data about him or her is held on a computer file;

— to have access to that information;

— if it is incorrect, to have it corrected;

— if appropriate, to have it erased.

— *an individual shall be entitled to be informed whether data is held of which he or she is the subject.* This is subject to the exemptions considered in Chapter 7.

By an "individual", the law is referring to a natural person, not a body corporate or the person who happens to be holding a particular public office if the information would apply equally to *anyone* who held that office.

The paradox of having to be sure of the identity of the person applying for information (and thus making that individual divulge *additional* personal information) is interesting and under-emphasised. To be safe from multiplying personal data unnecessarily, and from holding data *about* personal data, which might itself be regarded as personal data, do not record on any computer file the fact of any application for such information.

"Data", according to the law[1], "means information recorded in a form in which it can be processed by equipment operating automatically in response to instructions given for that purpose". "Processing", in relation to data, likewise[2] "means amending, augmenting, deleting or rearranging the data or extracting the information constituting

[1] S.1(2)
[2] S.1(7)

the data and, in the case of personal data, means performing any of those operations *by reference to the data subject"* (my italics).

All this has two important implications:

— "data" about which its subject has a right of access *includes* printed reports and microfiche/microfilm *only if* you have equipment (eg an optical character reader) which enables such output *to be read and further processed as part of the same computer program or interrelated set of programs*, and *not otherwise*. If, once data has been printed out, it would have to be re-input through an intermediate process (eg manual keying), it has ceased to be within the scope of the legislation as far as it deals with rights of subject access. *This does not apply to disclosure of information to others* (see Chapter 7);

— data which is processed otherwise than "by reference to the data subject" is excluded from the operation of the law. Thus data *used in straightforward word processing* is excluded, even when this includes words containing personal information about an identifiable individual. The law itself states[1] that it does not apply to "any operation performed only for the purpose of preparing the text of documents". This seems to reveal a lack of understanding, by the legal draughtsmen, that it is not an "operation" but software which is directed towards certain purposes, and that both data processing and word processing can be carried out by pieces of software which are integrated. This lack of understanding is worrying, but does not affect the exclusion of word processing files from the ambit of the law.

Data used in ordinary data processing is also excluded, even when the data includes personal information, *provided that the personal information is incidental to the processing* (eg patent data including, incidentally, the inventor's name; or a professional time recording and client billing system).

[1] S.1(8)

Your obligations in respect of an application by a data subject are considered in Chapter 3. Even if a person only applies for information about *whether* personal data about him or her is held on your computer files, you must give access to the information itself if there is any. It is almost certain, however, that in any such case the person will also ask to have access to such information anyway;

— *an individual shall be entitled to have access to data of which that individual is the subject.* The same principles apply as just set out above. You must supply the data by means of "a copy in writing of the information constituting such personal data". This wording is significant. You cannot avoid the requirement to supply an individual with relevant personal information simply because data is held in coded form (through the use of indicators or otherwise). The law makes it quite clear that if it "is expressed in terms which are not intelligible without explanation", then you must provide the explanation as well as the data itself[1];

— *an individual shall be entitled to have personal data, of which he or she is the subject, corrected if it is incorrect.* This is clearly a principle to which everyone would subscribe, although in practice there may be problems of interpretation if value judgements are involved. Use objective data if you can (Mr. X is 40 years old) rather than a generic classification (Mr. X is middle-aged);

— *an individual shall be entitled to have personal data, of which he or she is the subject, erased if appropriate.* This would apply if, for example, data were being held longer than necessary, or if it were not relevant to the purpose for which its user purported to be holding it.

Note that "erased" means physically deleted, not just marked with an indicator as "deleted" – whether then accessible by application programs or not. *If a record can be accessed at all*, even if only through system software and even if only by a systems support specialist, it will not have been "deleted" for the purpose of adherence to this principle.

[1] S.21(1)

Principle 8 (see also Principle 5) – Appropriate security measures shall be taken against:

— unauthorised access to data;

— unauthorised alteration of data (N.B. For some reason, unauthorised primary input – insertion – of data onto a computer is not directly mentioned in this set of principles, but must be regarded as implicit in this one);

— unauthorised (including accidental) destruction of data;

— unauthorised disclosure of data;

— accidental loss of data;

and to ensure that data remains accurate and up-to-date.

These principles (as opposed to Principles 4 and 6) are the most significant requirements, now incorporated into law at least in respect of personal data, for the implementation of controls over data processing. They entail the implementation of an integrated set of controls, including user controls, programmed controls and computer installation controls, over:

— input;

— processing and output;

— master files and permanent and semi-permanent reference data.

Such controls, taken together, should be designed to minimise the risk of either accidental or deliberate error in the data to be processed, the processing itself, the results of the processing and how they are used.

These principles are inextricably interrelated.

INPUT CONTROLS

Input controls are necessary to ensure that for each significant type of data input for processing:

— the input is authorised (if considered necessary for that input) and at the level of responsibility considered appropriate;

— significant elements of input are complete;

— significant elements of input are accurate.

There should normally therefore be controls over input, which might in many cases be effected by means of teleprocessing, but which nevertheless might involve the batching of data input, and the maintenance of accepted batched items on separate files until they can be used to update the main records.

Systems should also normally include validation checks on input, such as:

— matching input streams before data is used for updating;

— use of sequential reference numbers for data input;

— verification of the presence on master files of data relevant to particular updates;

— combination, format, completeness and reasonableness validation.

The design of clerical control procedures which are to be incorporated into a system using a computer application, to ensure that what has been processed constitutes all the information which is relevant to the field of accounting concerned, is often left until a very late stage in the development of a computer application, and sometimes deferred until after live running of the application has begun. Very often, the deferment of such procedures leads to a situation in which they are never properly defined at all, and where the actual procedures put into effect are much less effective than those which were originally anticipated, causing mounting problems as the processing of data continues.

At one time, much of the necessary detailed control work tended to be carried out by members of the data processing staff in a more or less well-defined data control department. However, there has for a long time been a realisation that control over important and sensitive computer applications ought properly to be carried out by the system users, who do not necessarily have detailed knowledge of the type of data concerned.

As systems have increased in complexity, and as the use of teleprocessing devices has become more widespread, the realisation that control ought not to be left to data processing personnel has continued. But it is not always realised how greatly the means of implementing such control have been modified, and in some cases have all but disappeared.

For example, input to medical records or tax records from terminals located in several different parts of geographically separated hospitals or tax offices might well bring about a situation where no single control or data administration department could exercise effective control over the insertion of a new record onto a file at any particular moment. This is partly because it is virtually impossible to impose the same uniform set of control standards at every remote terminal concerned. It may well be difficult, therefore, to provide for the necessary combination of clerical and programmed validation controls to ensure that records are not introduced, deleted or altered in an unauthorised or incorrect manner.

It should be emphasised that in certain instances where data is collected on-line from a number of separate locations, there may in fact be no control over input to ensure that it is complete and that data rejected by the validation programs are corrected and resubmitted. In such instances, greater attention should be given to other aspects of control – for example, to control over output.

PROCESSING AND OUTPUT CONTROLS

These are required to ensure that:

— the processing remains accurate in respect of each significant calculation or exception condition;

and to ensure that for each significant output report or file:

— each particular aspect of output is complete and accurate;

— each physical output item is properly distributed;

— each output item (whether printed or displayed on screen) is used as intended.

There should thus normally be controls over processing (for example, verification by program that control information derived from access to all the records via one index is equivalent to that via all the others). It may be possible for this control to be related to, for example, a clerical system of accounting controls, but even if not, it should still be performed. There should normally be controls to ensure the proper distribution and adequate examination and scrutiny of all significant tabulations produced as output from a computer system. Very often, it will be found that such controls can be exercised centrally, in relation to detailed tabulations of information which has been processed at an earlier time, by means of some form of clerical scrutiny; in many cases, and ideally, by reference to exception reports.

There is no reason why, if such control procedures are implemented with the appropriate degree of forethought, they should not be both effective and useful. *However, if they are ill-defined, or the clerical procedures which are imposed are not properly interrelated with programmed controls, clerical control work will be ineffective.* The systems development work undertaken in incorporating the programmed controls into the application, and in designing the tabulations to be used in such clerical procedures, will also have been largely wasted. Most damaging of all, the system will not only be uncontrolled but, *while being uncontrolled, will be believed to be controlled.* In such an environment, it is possible for considerable quantities of assets to be lost or misappropriated, for very misleading management information to be produced, and for personal and other restricted data to be disseminated more widely than intended or permitted.

FILE CONTROLS

These are required to ensure that for each significant data file containing reference or summarised accounting information:

— data on the file is authorised, complete, and accurate;

— the correct version of the file is used in all aspects of processing.

The specification of file controls will require consideration to be given to the maintenance of the consistency of the database with the real world. This entails the proper performance of the functions of data administration (see Chapter 3).

The use of database systems necessarily implies a far greater degree of formality in the specification and the documentation of the data held in each of the sub-files and fields within a database.

Do not just stop when you have located inconsistency between items of data on your computer files, and determined by what breach of control it became possible for such inconsistency to exist. Ask *why* that control was supposed to be there in the first place – what attitudes of mind does its breach indicate, and are those attitudes justified? In other words, is the control tacitly recognised to be irrelevant? And if it is not, what really relevant problem was the ignored control originally intended to address? And is that ultimately relevant problem, to which the official control is tacitly recognised to be irrelevant, actually addressed by any *other* control?

For example, ask your credit controller whether he/she actually *uses* the information on credit control produced by your computer system. If not, why is the data, or the relevant program, retained? In the context of data protection, the short odds are that it purports to be private information, that it is wrong, that you could therefore be in big trouble with it, and *yet that ultimately you do not need it at all*!

If it is discovered that data has for some reason been lost – and this discovery may result from a disagreement of control totals or a breakdown of processing controls, or the absence or incongruity of alphabetic data on file – then it must be possible to have access to an earlier version of the file or database concerned. This begs the question how often it is reasonable to delete a file or reorganise a database and what back-up copies should be kept.

The decisions to be made depend on the following considerations:

— how crucial it is to recover immediately (in which case very frequent copies will probably be the answer);

— the amount of storage capacity available for retention of files copied;

— the processing time available for large-scale re-processing;

— the implication of suspending on-line working while

dumps are taken, or of degrading on-line working while parts of a database are copied;

— the effectiveness of the method used to log files which are backed-up.

Particular attention should therefore be given to:

— *Procedures* to ensure that:

— it is not possible for any file to be excluded from regular security copying procedures;

— such copies are maintained in at least two separate locations (one near the computer in order to be available at once if something goes wrong with the file being processed, and one at a remote site in case there is a fire or comparable catastrophe);

— the exact impact of these procedures is taken into account at the time of the specification of each individual application which is to use the data concerned (so that, where appropriate, additional procedures may be applied in relation to a specific application to ensure the level of back-up required by the users of that application only);

— adequate checkpoint procedures are instituted, particularly where databases are used in conjunction with teleprocessing, to ensure that if corruption of the database takes place during any particular session of transaction processing, the status of the database before that processing began may be reconstructed, and the appropriate transactions re-applied.

— *Circumstances in which items of data on a database may come to be locked.* Programs should not be permanently locked out of a database, or any part of it, by other programs. In any case, users should be quite clear what technical processes are involved when an access attempt is made to a field which is locked either by another program or because of the characteristics of that field specified in its data description.

— *Appropriate use of levels of access security which may be available*. These include:

— keys to restrict access to files (eg passwords, used in conjunction with teleprocessing), to identify users of applications and the files under their direct control, and where possible the type of operation (eg updating) to be carried out;

— locks included within the data descriptions of certain types of record, to prevent particular types of operation on the contents of those records, either completely or without use of a further password.

You should ensure, at the system design stage, that you are aware what access key facilities are available, and the uses which are to be made of them.

— *The possibility of answering time-dependent questions that should be considered in relation to all items of data which are of special importance*:

— what was the value of field X at time t?

— over what time-span did field X have the value v?

— what program made reference to, or updated, field X at time t?

— what user at what terminal submitted transaction Y at time t?

— is it possible to reproduce exactly the sequence of operations which have updated a file since the last, arbitrarily determined, time at which that file was considered complete and accurate?

If a series of values can be included in the file to indicate the time of the last change of each significant field, so much the better, but there should always be some means, direct or indirect, of obtaining the answers to such questions.

PARADOXES OF LEGISLATION FOR DATA PROTECTION

There are certainly some interesting flaws in one of the rights conferred by the Data Protection law; that the individual to whom it relates shall be legally entitled to see it, check it and if necessary have it corrected or erased.

In order to exercise this right of access one first has to prove one's identity (see section 21(4) of the Data Protection Act). But this can only be done either by the use of a state-allocated identity number or a state-controlled address (the acceptance of which in other democratic countries simply proves how badly the concept of personal privacy travels) or by the provision, to the data user or to a court, of additional personal information – which is then available to be recorded (possibly wrongly again) on further computer files. This is a paradox which arises from making a public issue of privacy.

Even if this problem can be satisfactorily overcome, another one remains. What the exercise of a right of access will generate is a printout[1], purporting to include all the information relating to the individual concerned. But surely this is the very information which ought to be regarded with the greatest suspicion of all. For the fact that a piece of information is not printed on a particular occasion does not prove that it has been deleted from the relevant computer files – only that its tabulation on that occasion has been inhibited.

And good technical control of computer operations and systems development does not imply legitimate use of the data processed. Indeed it may actually make it easier, if thought appropriate, to conceal the extent of any misuse. This is a paradox which arises from the lack of any necessary identity between the objectives and the techniques of data control.

Current methods of data storage, in any event, certainly seem to encourage the development of data correlation itself. An ideal database is rightly perceived as a model of the relationships between entities in the real world, and the programs which update and retrieve data from that database as models of events in the world. Since it is likely that more and more personal information will be recorded on such databases, it is apparently inevitable that the aspect of the world which they will particularly come to reflect will be the unity of items of information about particular individu-

[1] The same considerations would apply equally to a video display.

als. Technically, this strand of concern about the continuing development of computer processing systems could be expressed as being that an individual person is an ideal subject for representation at the apex of an information hierarchy. And that currently unconnected information hierarchies may in due course be linked through this ideal common point of reference to create bigger and better hierarchies.

If this is recognised, it presents us with a simple means of exploding these anxieties. It is not technically necessary to process data in this way. It is not even necessarily convenient. All that is required, to minimise the possibility of misuse of information recorded on computer files, is that in no circumstances should that information be associated with an index or identifiable sequence of personal identification codes.

This would not appear to inhibit the recording in computer files of any special categories of information, nor to affect any legitimate function of a self-contained information system. It would also appear to be a reasonably easy condition to monitor without the need for an oppressive monitoring agency.

It would, of course, be difficult to give people access to data recorded about them under these conditions. But this would then be so much less important: the need for a right of access to data, by the person about whom it is recorded (whether on computer files or otherwise), is a direct function of the extent to which that data is already readily available to others. The best way to maximise the privacy of data may thus be to make it hard to get at – for anyone.

Assuming that the use of database systems continues to increase, however (in connection with the use of both large and small computers), the need to address the problem more directly remains.

CONTROLS APPROPRIATE TO SYSTEMS USING DATABASES

The following main headings are suggested, in respect of which there should be satisfactory specific controls (including, where appropriate, specified standards to which adherence should be required):

— *Physical security*

    (a) Computers (mainframes, minis, stand-alone micros and intelligent terminals);

        (i)   Site security;

        (ii)   Restriction of permitted access;

    (b) Terminals (where appropriate);

        (i)   Site security;

        (ii)   Restriction of permitted access;

    (c) Printed output.

— *Security of access to computer via terminal (where applicable)*

    (a) Security by password (access key), to ensure user validity;

        (i)   Procedures;

        (ii)   Logging and reporting of access attempts;

    (b) Message transmission controls, and the reporting back of;

        (i)   Confirmation of messages received and queued for processing;

        and

        (ii)   Errors in transmission of messages;

        (iii)   Action to be taken in the event of transmission errors;

        (iv)   Procedures for testing of these facilities (eg by internal auditors).

— *File security*

    (a) Protection by passwords, of particular databases, to ensure access to those files only by authorised persons;

    (b) Protection by passwords, of particular functions (eg

updating), to ensure that they are carried out only by authorised persons;

(c) Operating controls; eg,

    (i)   logging and reporting of jobs run;

    (ii)   protection of intermediate files awaiting printing.

— *File storage and back-up*

(a) Retention of files on and off site;

(b) Procedures for cataloguing files;

(c) Procedures for cataloguing operational programs and previous versions of programs.

— *Standby facilities*

(a) Procedures for batch processing during unavailability of full facilities;

(b) Procedures for reversion to other procedures during prolonged unavailability of processing capability; eg,

    — manual procedures;

    — transfer to another installation.

— *Operating standards and procedures*

— *Duties and responsibilities of technical support group*

— *Procedures for the implementation of new applications using each database*

(a) Procedures for appraisal of proposed new projects;

(b) Liaison with users and resolution of requirements of different users;

(c) Procedures for testing of programs and program amendments;

(d) Procedures for updating information.

— *Documentation of standards for use*

(a) by database administration;

(b) by application users;

(c) by computer operators;

(d) by technical support group;

(e) by systems analysts and programmers.

N.B. 1 – re passwords

Controls should be implemented in relation to:

(a) responsibility for maintenance of records, and issues, of passwords;

(b) circumstances under which they will be changed;

(c) details of availability of, and control over, privileged access (eg by software support specialists) to password files;

(d) procedures for deletion of intermediate files (including print image files and data queue files).

N.B. 2 – re database administration

Documentation should include details of:

(a) specified levels of control and control priorities;

(b) all data specifications (schemas and sub-schemas) used within the database system;

(c) all file and record access locks incorporated within any of the data specifications.

NETWORKS

In this connection, developments in communications, and corresponding developments in facilities available to the users of those systems, have permitted the extensive use of minicomputer and microcomputer systems as terminals for the entry and retrieval of information.

Firstly, the use of such equipment has permitted the distribution to users, sometimes in widely-separated locations, of:

— immediate access to information from the files of a large
  central computer;

— the ability to update and amend their own data files;

— their own data processing capability (distributed intellig-
  ence, whether with the ability to use data from the central
  files or not).

Secondly, such equipment provides excellent scope for access by
such users to a data network, where all users are linked to all
others. This may incorporate the use of a computer with the role of
controlling the network (the System Network Architecture
approach), and providing a focus for the technical expertise necessary to support it.

It may also, however, incorporate no such control computer, and
there is great scope for the development of local area networks,
operating within a limited physical area such as an office or a
factory. Such networks – in principle – enable a terminal, a
minicomputer or indeed a mainframe simply to be plugged in and
begin communicating with others already attached.

The control principles for networks (whether distributed or
local) are clear up to a point. Determine the purpose of the
network, the nature and sensitivity of messages which are to be
passed through it, and seek the degree of control appropriate to
those criteria. If accounting information, personal data, authority
to receive funds or other assets, or other sensitive material, is being
transmitted over a network, then

— the individual terminals and other equipment attached to
  the network must be adequately controlled;

— control must be exercised to restrict access to and use of:

    — the modems and communications controllers (if it is a
      distributed network);

    — dial-up procedures using public telephone lines (if
      applicable);

    — private communications lines;

    — local cables.

The relevant control may be necessary in relation to hardware, physical communications lines and (where relevant) the software used on the central computer to control the network. It may not always be at all easy to determine which is most vulnerable, or which has been compromised in the event of a violation of the system. A great deal of technical knowledge may therefore be required for these purposes. The logging of communications, by both transmitter and receiver, and the monitoring of the logs and follow-up of apparent discrepancies, becomes particularly important in such circumstances.

However, no complete philosophy for the control of communications networks as a whole has yet been evolved. Treating them as a collection of separate parts, and controlling each of those parts separately, will only be partially satisfactory, and then only if it is done analytically. On the other hand the number of possible methods of putting a network together is so great that each case must to some extent be evaluated on its own merits.

7 Protecting Special Types of Data

EXEMPTIONS FROM RIGHTS OF ACCESS

Normally, a person has the right (under the seventh protection principle incorporated into the law) to be given access to computer-maintained data of which he or she is the subject, and to have it corrected or erased if it is incorrect. (As mentioned above, it must be supposed that by "erased" the law means physical deletion, not just the addition of an indicator that the record is no longer to be processed as part of the live system.)

However, this right is not available if the data is held for any of the following purposes:

— national security (as certified by a Minister of the Crown);

— the prevention or detection of crime and the apprehension or prosecution of offenders;

— the assessment or collection of any tax or duty;

— keeping various health and social security records (to be specified by the Home Secretary);

— making judicial appointments;

— any system which the Home Secretary may specifically exempt (particularly to help prevent fraud);

— only for statistical or research purposes, and not otherwise revealed.

There are six other restrictions of the right of access to data, and they are very important. They apply to data held:

— *only* for the purpose of calculating pay or pensions (thus including statutory sick pay calculations, but *not* personnel records), including payments in kind and gratuities;

  N.B. 1: It must be presumed that calculation of pay extends to calculation of employer's national health contributions.

  N.B. 2: If you are keeping personnel records, you are exempt (section 1(3)) from any requirement to give an individual employee access to any record of your intentions towards that employee (eg he is not to be promoted). This does not apply to "expressions of opinion" about an employee (eg he is incompetent) – so ensure that you are very clear about which is which.

— *only* for the purpose of keeping accounts relating to business or other activities, or records of purchases, sales or other transactions, to ensure correct payments or receipts;

— *only* in connection with the management of the personal, family, household or recreational affairs of an *individual*. This exemption was included to remove the files of home computer users from the practical effects of the law. Such users are still theoretically bound by the data protection principles themselves, which are enacted in a part of the law from which no-one, strictly speaking, is exempt – in other words, even home computer users are supposed to have residual regard to these principles;

— by an "unincorporated members' club" (eg a commune, chess club, amateur dramatic society, residents' association, local church or the office sweepstake) and relating *only* to the members of that "club". N.B. This exemption does *not* apply if the records include information about others who are not "club" members. Also, all members *must be specifically asked* whether they object to the maintenance of personal data about them by the "club".

  Data must not be so held, *unless the data user registers* under the Data Protection law, about any member who objects.

N.B. This is a somewhat tortured provision, but no doubt it will suffice for its purpose;

— for the purpose of distributing or recording the distribution of "articles" (eg mail shots) or information to individuals, and consisting of their names and addresses *only*. Again, all potential recipients *must be asked specifically* if they object to the maintenance of their names and addresses on computer file for this purpose. Data must not be so held, *unless the data user registers* under the Data Protection law, about anyone who objects;

— in respect of a claim to legal professional privilege. Your dealings with your legal adviser, notwithstanding some continuing reservations by the Law Society about the adequacy of this provision, remain as confidential as ever.

Provided that your system does not explicitly fall under one of these headings, you should reconcile yourself to complying with any reasonable requests when people:

— ask to know whether information is held about them;

— ask to know what it is.

Make sure they pay their fees before you tell them (the maximum fees payable will be set from time to time by the Registrar). And make sure that they are who they say they are.

An application to know *whether* information is held, *and* to have access to such information if any, only counts as a single application for the purposes of payment – in any case the former must be deemed (see section 21(2)) to incorporate the latter.

EXTENT OF EXEMPTIONS FROM RIGHTS OF ACCESS

Normally, the exemption only extends as far as the right of access itself. The data subject *still has the right to have erroneous data corrected or erased, and to apply to the Court for this to be done, and for damages if loss has been suffered*, provided that the data subject is aware of the contents of the data from some other source. However, this does not apply to:

— national security records;

— payroll records;

— accounting records;

— personal, family, household and recreational records;

— club records and agreed mailing group records.

No-one other than the data user has any rights whatsoever in respect of the correctness or otherwise of these types of record. This *also* applies to data which is already legally required to be made publicly available (eg records of membership of limited companies): this is because there are *separate* procedures for access to and rectification of such records.

EXEMPTIONS FROM NON-DISCLOSURE REQUIREMENTS

A data user must thus disclose personal data to a data subject unless there is an exemption from this requirement. Conversely, a data user normally must *not* disclose personal data to anyone *other* than the person to whom that data refers. However, this requirement does not apply if the data is disclosed in any of the following circumstances:

— to comply with a Court Order, or to get legal advice;

— to enable the Registrar or the Data Protection Tribunal (the appeals body) to carry out their functions;

— to protect national security;

— to facilitate, or not to prejudice, the prevention or detection of crime or the apprehension or prosecution of offenders, or the assessment or collection of any tax or duty;

— in the course of calculating pay or pensions, amounts due may be disclosed to a bank, so that the bank can pay them into employees' bank accounts, or to actuaries;

— in respect of accounting records, for the purpose of audit, or giving information about the data *user's* financial affairs;

— if the data relates *only* to personal, family, household or recreational affairs of an individual;

— if the data relates *only* to members of private "clubs", as defined above – but only in respect of members who do not object. All members must be asked if they object or not;

— if the data is *only* names and addresses held for the purpose of distributing or recording the distribution of articles to those individuals – but only in respect of individuals who do not object. All those concerned must be asked if they object or not;

— if the data subject has requested or consented to the disclosure;

— if the disclosure is urgently required to prevent injury or other damage to the health of any person, or if it is required for certain health research purposes;

— if the disclosure is required under any other existing law.

Note that you are *not obliged* to disclose data for any of these reasons, except compliance with a Court Order or existing law: you are simply given the right to do so if you wish.

Section 1(9) of the Data Protection law states that "disclosing", in relation to data, includes disclosing information extracted from the data. This appears to *include* printouts of data in the scope of the law.

This also applies to computer output onto microfiche, microfilm of computer tabulations or any other form in which information, extracted from computer records, may be stored after it has been extracted. In other words any item of personal data which has once been through a computer system, or been calculated or derived from the use of such a system, even after it has been removed from magnetic records, must not be disclosed – except to the subject of that data or in accordance with one or more of the above exemptions.

EXEMPTION FROM REGISTRATION

You do not have to register as a data user under the Data Protection Act:

— if your data does not include any personal data;

— if your systems are certified by a senior Minister of the Crown as being for the purpose of national security;

— in respect of your systems for calculating payroll and pensions (*provided that* you do not disclose the data to anyone except the payee, someone else who is actually going to pay the money (eg your bank), your auditors or actuaries, anyone whom the payee has agreed should be given the information (eg a pension fund trustee), or otherwise for the purpose of giving information about *your own* financial affairs);

— in respect of your accounting and stock recording systems, *provided that* you do not disclose the data to anyone except your auditors, or for the purpose of giving information about *your own* financial affairs;

— in respect of your own personal, family, household or recreational systems;

— in respect of unincorporated members' "clubs", *again* provided the data *only* relates to club members who, having been asked, have not objected to the data being held;

— in respect of *only* names and addresses held in connection with distributing things to people, *again* provided that the individuals concerned, having been asked, have not objected to the data being held;

— if the data consists of information which you are obliged to disclose under the terms of any other law (eg registers of limited companies).

You are still, however, expected to have regard to the data protection principles.

N.B. Users of police and criminal investigation systems are *not* exempt from registration. They *may* be exempt from the application of *certain* of the powers of the Registrar under *certain* circumstances, as may governmental systems (see S.37).

Use of a computer which is physically located in another country does not provide a means of exemption from the requirements of the Data Protection law in respect of personal data, if the user (the one who "controls" the data) is

— resident in the UK, and

— uses or intends to use the data in the UK.

In other words, if you reside here and process your data overseas, but access it via a terminal in this country, or receive reports extracted from it, then you are still required to register under, and you are subject to all the other obligations of, this law.

Conversely, if personal data is processed in the UK, but the person who "holds" that data is genuinely resident outside the UK (as, for example, in the case of the UK branch of a multi-national group), it is still almost certain that the Registrar will interpret the law so that it applies to the servant or agent of that person in the UK. (The necessary authority appears to be contained in section 38(3) of the law.) The details of the person who is the servant or agent concerned will have to be registered.

OTHER RESTRICTIONS ON PROCESSING

Normally in any other case, if you have registered your use of personal data, you may process it without further concern. However, the Home Secretary can (and perhaps should) impose additional safeguards and restrictions on processing data about:

— racial origins;

— political opinions;

— religious or other beliefs;

— physical or mental health;

— sexual attitudes and orientations;

— criminal convictions.

In any case, it is best not to hold records of this sort[1] if you can

---

[1] It is open to question exactly how far information in respect of some of these categories (which are derived directly from the European Convention on the Protection of Individuals with regard to Automatic Processing of Personal Data) can be inferred from other information without being recorded directly. Followers of Sherlock Holmes will be aware how revealing are the inferences which can sometimes be drawn from the most trifling pieces of evidence – *even without the help of computers*.

possibly avoid it, as they are sure to be regarded as provocative. If it is inevitable, make special efforts to ensure that the data is correct: otherwise you may have a libel suit on your hands, as well as the Registrar on your back.

8 Mitigating the Effects of Legislation

There are certain actions which you can take to mitigate the practical effects of data protection legislation, while complying with the spirit of it, to ensure that people are not unnecessarily alarmed by the possibilities of wrongly manipulating personal information held on computer files. Some suggestions are as follows:

— Simply keep personal records by means of clerical systems. You will then be completely exempt from any requirement to comply with the Data Protection Act. You could even find, in some cases, that it is less costly and less irritating. A card index of personnel records is often just as powerful a data storage and look-up medium as a computerised personnel system.

— If you hold a lot of personal information a great deal depends (as already noted in Chapter 6) on how you organise your systems. For example, if you use an integrated database it will be possible to register its use in connection with a unified set of purposes. If you do so, you will be committed (subject to the exemptions already noted) to telling anyone who applies to you, on payment of a single fee (yet to be decided), whether he or she is the subject of any item of data on that database – and providing a copy of the relevant information, if any. If you use a database it will probably be relatively easy to comply with such requirements, because the information will be easily accessible. You will probably be able to state whether there is an entity on that database containing reference to that person's name or some other record of identity, and to identify all other entities on the database with which it is linked or related. Nevertheless, it could still be an oppressive financial burden.

However, if you register your systems as application-based (eg as separate personnel, payroll and pensions systems) – in other words state separately all the purposes for which you hold data – you will be able (section 21(3)) to require a separate fee for each request for access to information.

Of course, if you *have* application-based systems using, say, hundreds of magnetic tapes or diskettes, you really must register separate purposes for holding data anyway, otherwise the financial burden could be intolerable. But there is nothing to stop you doing so in relation to the use of an integrated database as well – even though the same physical data is used in the processing of all the applications.

— All computer applications should be designed in such a way as to identify and segregate data which needs to be protected – either because it is personal data or because it is sensitive in some other way (eg it is a record of a loan or of a valuable stock item in a warehouse). This can bring significant advantages. For example, the most positive response to data disclosure requirements may be to hold your records of persons' names and addresses on files or databases which are physically separate from your other files and databases.

This also makes sense from the point of view of processing efficiency and ease of updating. Link each personal name and address record with other records via an identification key which is unique to your system and which is not based on any element of the person's name or any other personal data (eg birth date). The physical disk address location of the record would do quite nicely for this purpose. Such an identification key, in itself, *is not a piece of personal information*. Thus its appearance in other records containing personal information, but without names and addresses, does *not* make those records relate to an individual "who can be identified from the information" – and thus could well, given certain other conditions, remove them from the application of the Data Protection law altogether.

These other conditions would have to include procedures to ensure that those of your personnel, normally having access to name and address records, did not have access to any other records, and vice versa. Then the records would be administratively and logically, as well as physically, separate, and you would be able to transfer or disclose your records (except the actual name and address records themselves) without breaking any of the provisions of the legislation. The name and address records themselves would be registered as being held for the purpose of communicating with those individuals, or simply as a personnel record.

There is, however, no way to avoid the right of any person to be given access to computer-maintained information of which he or she is the subject, and to have it corrected or erased if it is wrong. *This applies even if part of the information which identifies such a person is not maintained on a computer file but is "other information in the possession of the data user" (S.1(3)).*

This is the essence of the law to protect personal data: the data must be both true and fairly processed.

Bibliography

Accounting Software Controls: a Guidance Document, NCC Publications, 1983.

Consultative Committee of Accountancy Bodies' Auditing Practices Committee, *Auditing in a Computer Environment*, January 1982.

Data Protection Bill, HMSO, published 1983, as amended.

Data Protection: the Government Proposals for Legislation, HMSO, Cmnd. 8539; April 1982 – incorporating the European Convention for the Protection of Individuals with Regard to the Automatic Processing of Personal Data.

Deloitte Haskins & Sells and the National Computing Centre; Computer Security Series, *The External Auditor as Privacy Inspector*, NCC Publications, 1982.

European Convention for the Protection of Individuals with Regard to Automatic Processing of Personal Data, Transnational Data Report, North Holland/Transnational Data Reporting Service Inc, Washington, March 1981.

G L Simons, *Privacy in the Computer Age*, NCC Publications, 1982.

Infotech State of the Art Report (Series 8, No. 8), *Computer Audit and Control*, Infotech Ltd, 1980.

OECD Guidelines Governing the Protection of Privacy and Transborder Flows of Personal Data, Transnational Data Report,

North Holland/Transnational Data Reporting Service Inc, Washington, January 1981.

Report of the Committee on Data Protection, HMSO, Cmnd. 7341, the "Lindop Report", December 1978.

Report of the Committee on Privacy, HMSO, Cmnd. 5012, the "Younger Report", July 1972.

Index

73